The Ultimate Wedding Checklist

Your Essential Guide to Planning the Perfect Day

Brenda S. Cornelius

Copyright © 2024 by Brenda S. Cornelius

All rights reserved.
No part of this publication may be reproduced, stored in a retrieval system, or transmitted, in any form or by any means, electronic, mechanical, photocopying, recording, or otherwise, without the prior permission of the copyright owner.

Contents

Introduction

A young couple who were incredibly in love once resided in a little town that was surrounded by endless fields of wildflowers and rolling hills. Their aspirations entwined, their hearts beat in unison, and they felt that their love story was meant to be something truly remarkable. However, one very important occasion was approaching: their wedding day.

Nowadays, weddings are meant to be the pinnacle of celebration and love, a day full of happiness, pleasure, and treasured memories. However, for our couple - let's call them Emily and Alex - the mere thought of planning their dream wedding sent shivers down their spines. They were disoriented and overwhelmed by the amount of choices they had to make, details to arrange, and deadlines to fulfill.

Do not worry, though, as Emily and Alex are not traveling alone. They have discovered a book of magic, a goldmine of knowledge and direction that will turn their stressful wedding preparations into a happily ever after. My friends, this book is called **"The Ultimate Wedding Checklist: Your Essential Guide to Planning the Perfect Day."**

Turning the pages of this enchanted book will take you on an engrossing journey full of laughter, love, and priceless insights. Accompany Emily and Alex as they negotiate the complicated routes of wedding preparation, picking up insightful knowledge and unearthing treasures along the process.

However, allow me to introduce myself before we go right into the realm of wedding planning. I'm [Brenda S. Cornelius], and I'll be your reliable guide on this enchanted adventure. I am a seasoned wedding planner with years of experience arranging romantic events, and I am here to offer my knowledge, advice, and insider knowledge with you in order to help you create the wedding of your dreams.

All the information you want to arrange the ideal wedding will be covered in the upcoming chapters, from determining your budget and venue to picking the appropriate dress and creating a ceremony that tells the tale of your love. You will find insightful analysis, useful suggestions, and motivational tales with every page turn that will enable you to design a wedding day that is entirely your own.

But there's still more! Along with the priceless knowledge contained within these pages, there is a wealth of information available to help you along the way. These helpful resources, which range from vendor contact lists and example schedules to planning worksheets and checklists, will keep you focused, organized, and stress-free throughout the planning process.

Are you prepared to go out on a once-in-a-lifetime trip, dear reader?

Are you prepared to make your ideal wedding a reality?

If so, take hold of this enchanted book and start your adventure. We shall make memories that will last a lifetime and laugh and weep together. This is "The Ultimate Wedding Checklist: Your Essential Guide to Planning the Perfect Day." Now let the magic start!

Chapter 1

Getting Started

Every love tale starts with a dream—a picture of a world full of joy, laughter, and unending love. And that dream was about to come true for Emily and Alex. They knew that their "happily ever after" was about to start as they sat hand in hand and looked into one other's eyes. But there was one enormous chore ahead of them: organizing the ideal wedding. Only then could they walk down the aisle and say "**I do.**"

Emily and Alex were caught up in a frenzy of excitement and expectation as the sun set and the stars started to shine in the night sky. They didn't know where to start, but they had always imagined a wedding that would be as special and lovely as their love tale. They were feeling overwhelmed and indecisive about where to begin, with so many choices to make and things to arrange.

Nevertheless, readers need not worry, since Emily and Alex are not traveling alone. They have discovered a book of magic, a goldmine of knowledge and direction that will turn their stressful wedding preparations into a happily ever after.

Let's set off on this fascinating adventure together as we solve the puzzles around wedding preparation and learn how to create a day that is just as remarkable and enchanted as Emily and Alex's love.

Understanding Your Vision

To begin creating the ideal wedding, you must first understand your vision. Which type of nuptials are your ideal ones? Is it a small, private get-together in a rural barn or a big event in an opulent ballroom? Shut your eyes and visualize the ideal day. What do you see? How do you feel? Just take a time to picture every little detail, down to the background music and the flowers on the tables. It is your wedding day, and it ought to represent your own love tale.

From the start, Emily and Alex had a clear vision for their project. They desired a sophisticated, charming, and romantic wedding with a dash of whimsy. Under a canopy of sparkling lights, surrounded by their closest friends and family, they imagined exchanging vows. As they started the next chapter of their life together, they imagined themselves laughing, dancing, and enjoying all night long beneath the stars.

Setting Your Budget

Setting your budget is a good idea if you have a clear idea of what your ideal day looks like. Weddings may be costly events, and it's simple to overspend on ostentatious details and elaborate décor. However, take a minute to sit down with your partner and talk about your money before you start spending. What is the budget that you have set aside for your wedding? Which things are most important to you? Which expenses are you prepared to cut back on and which ones are you ready to spend on?

Establishing a budget was a difficult undertaking for Emily and Alex. They did not want to begin their marriage drowning in debt, but they also did not want their wedding to be exquisite and unforgettable. They debated and crunched numbers for a long time before settling on a budget that worked for them. They decided to forgo some of the less necessary costs and focus on the aspects of their wedding that meant the most to them, including the photographer and the location.

Creating a Timeline

After deciding on a budget and establishing their vision, Emily and Alex were prepared to go on to the next phase of their wedding preparations: developing a schedule. There are a lot of intricate and time-consuming chores involved in wedding planning, and it's common to feel overburdened by them. But worry not reader; as you approach your big day, a well-made timetable may keep you focused and organized.

Decide on a date for your wedding first. This will guide you as you plan each step along the road and act as the anchor for your timeline. The remaining jobs should then be divided into digestible portions, with deadlines and milestones assigned to each. Make sure to account for unforeseen circumstances or last-minute problems by adding extra time, and don't hesitate to ask for assistance when you need it.

Making a timeline saved Emily and Alex's lives. They immediately understood that they needed a strategy to stay on course because there were so many moving pieces to coordinate. They established timelines for chores like selecting a location, hiring caterers, and distributing invites as part of their monthly milestone wedding preparation process. They experienced exhilaration and a sense of success as they passed each milestone, knowing that they were getting closer to their

ideal wedding.

Chapter 2
Essential Pre-Planning

With a steaming cup of coffee in hand and the warm morning light streaming through the curtains, Emily and Alex were at the kitchen table, prepared to take on the next stage of their wedding preparations. They were excited to start **Chapter 2: Essential Pre-Planning,** still reeling from the exhilaration of **Chapter 1.**

Choosing Your Wedding Style and Theme

The first pre-planning task for Emily and Alex was deciding on their wedding theme and style. With so many options available, they felt overwhelmed and uncertain of where to begin. They wanted their wedding to be a representation of their distinct personalities and love story.

They were inundated with countless options as they perused Pinterest boards and bridal magazines: wacky garden parties, elegant black-tie events, rustic barn weddings, and everything in between. Which style was best for them, even if each had its own allure and charm?

After much thought and introspection, Emily and Alex decided on a theme of antique romance because it seemed authentic to who they were as a pair. They had visions of an elegant, timeless wedding with pastel colors and antique lace, a celebration of love evoking a bygone period.

Selecting the Perfect Venue

After deciding on their wedding theme and style, Emily and Alex's pre-planning checklist included choosing the ideal location. Finding a site that not only met their aesthetic vision but also suited their financial and logistical demands was crucial, as they understood that the venue would set the tone for their whole wedding day.

They browsed websites, read reviews, and compiled a list of possible locations while they searched the internet for suitable locations. They considered all of the options, analyzing the benefits and drawbacks of every choice, from elegant ballrooms to charming vineyards.

After physically seeing several locations and imagining their nuptials there, Emily and Alex eventually discovered the ideal location: a historic home tucked away in the countryside. Their stately ballroom, charming gardens, and expansive lawns provided the ideal setting for their vintage romance wedding.

Hiring Vendors: From Photographers to Caterers

After securing their site, Emily and Alex focused on selecting vendors to realize their vision. Vendors ranging from photographers to caterers, florists to DJs were available, each with their own set of skills and services.

They began by ranking their must-have suppliers, giving special attention to those whose offerings were critical to their plans for the day. While Alex was more concerned with getting a top-notch caterer to satisfy their guests' palates, Emily needed to locate the ideal photographer to capture every priceless moment.

They made contact with many vendors in each area, setting up meetings and consultations to talk about their goals, spending limits, and particular requirements. To make sure each vendor was a good fit for their wedding day, they carefully examined each vendor's portfolio, sought advice from friends and family, and read internet reviews.

Following weeks of discussions and planning, Emily and Alex eventually put together their ideal vendor team, carefully selecting each one to support the realization of their vision. They had put together a lineup of gifted experts who shared their enthusiasm for crafting wonderful moments, from the florist who would transform their venue with cascading blossoms to the DJ who would keep the dance floor filled all night long.

Chapter 3

The Bridal Party and Attire

The Bridal Party and Attire presented Emily and Alex with yet another thrilling chapter in their wedding preparation journey as the sun set and the stars started to shine in the night sky. Now that the location and suppliers had been confirmed, they could focus on the bridal party's outfits, which are among the most crucial elements of any wedding.

Choosing Your Wedding Reception Team

The selection of Emily and Alex's bridal party was the first task on their checklist. With so many friends and family members to pick from, they were faced with a tough decision as they prepared to start a new chapter of their life together and wanted the people closest to them to be by their side.

They began by compiling a list of possible applicants, taking suitability, proximity, and dependability into account. They wanted the members of their wedding party to be individuals who shared their enthusiasm for the big day and who not only loved and supported them but also got along well with one another.

Following much consideration and introspection, Emily and Alex decided on their wedding party: Alex would have his closest friend as his best man, and Emily would have her sister as her maid of honor. To add love and fun to their wedding party, they also carefully selected a few friends and family members to be bridesmaids and groomsmen.

Finding the Dress of Your Dreams

Finding the dress of her dreams was the next item on Emily's pre-wedding checklist after choosing their wedding party. Since she was a little child, she had fantasized about her wedding gown. She saw herself going down the aisle in a princess-worthy gown, and now that the big day was drawing near, she was eager to realize her dream.

She began by looking through Pinterest boards and bridal publications to gather ideas and inspiration for her ideal dress. In keeping with the old romance concept of her wedding, she knew she wanted something classic and exquisite. She pictured herself as a vision of elegance and beauty that would astound Alex as she glided down the aisle in a gown decorated with exquisite beading and delicate lace.

Equipped with her motivation, Emily embarked on a quest to discover the gown of her desires. She went to a lot of wedding stores and tried on gown after gown in an attempt to find "the one." She saw herself walking down the aisle, exchanging vows, and having a great time dancing with Alex at her side as she tried on each garment. Just as she was about to give up, she discovered the ideal outfit—a vision of tulle and lace that instantly transformed her into a real princess.

Attire for the Groom and Wedding Party

Alex was busy choosing the ideal outfit for himself and his groomsmen, while Emily was busy locating the dress of her dreams. In addition to making his wedding day ensemble fit Emily's dress and the antique romance concept of their celebration, he also wanted to remain loyal to his own sense of style.

He began by perusing alternatives ranging from traditional tuxedos to more laid-back suits both online and in local menswear stores. He thought about things like color, fabric, and fit, seeing himself and Emily standing at the altar looking sharp and fashionable in classic yet current clothing.

Alex tried on a number of different alternatives and, after considerable thought, decided on a traditional black tuxedo for himself and matching outfits for his groomsmen. As a reference to the romantic theme of their wedding, he opted for a light gray hue with delicate touches inspired by old styles. He accessorized with traditional black bow ties and leather shoes.

So, my dear readers, Emily, and Alex have taken a step closer to their ideal wedding day by selecting their bridal party and finding the dress of their dreams. But to successfully navigate the long and unpredictable path ahead, they will require all the assistance they can get.

Will they be able to pull off the ideal wedding, or will the obstacles in their way prove to be too much for them? Time will tell. But one thing is certain: everything is achievable with a lot of love and a tiny bit of magic.

Chapter 4

Invitations and Stationery

Emily and Alex were faced with yet another exciting phase in their wedding planning journey: stationery and invitations, while the gentle spring air fluttered through the trees and birds chirped happily in the background. Now that the bridal party and outfit had been decided upon, they could focus on one of the most crucial parts of planning a wedding: creating elegant invitations and stationery to set the tone for the big day.

Creating Your Invitations

Making their wedding invitations was the first task on Emily and Alex's invitation checklist. They wanted to leave a lasting impression as they knew that their invites would be the first chance their guests would see pictures on their wedding day.

They began by generating concepts for the design of their invitation, taking into account elements like color scheme, font, and general aesthetic. They wanted their invites to capture their distinct personalities and love stories, as well as the antique romantic aspect of their wedding.

Following a great deal of thought and searching for ideas, Emily and Alex ultimately decided on a design that reflected who they were as a pair. They went with a subdued color scheme of blush pink and gold, along with exquisite calligraphy and little flower flourishes. They decided on a traditional gatefold invitation, adding a little additional flair with a satin ribbon and a wax seal.

Guest List Management and RSVPs

Keeping track of their guest list and RSVPs was the next task on Emily and Alex's stationery checklist after designing and printing their invites. They were aware that arranging seats, catering, and other practical matters required keeping track of who was and wasn't attending.

First, they assembled a master guest list with names, addresses, and any other pertinent data. After that, they painstakingly hand-stamped each envelope and included a response card with pre-stamped envelopes so that visitors could RSVP when they sent out their invites.

A fresh set of obstacles presented itself to Emily and Alex when the RSVPs began to come in. While a few attendees swiftly sent in their RSVPs, others appeared to forget or take their time. They had to hunt down RSVPs that went missing, follow up with tardy respondents, and sometimes deal with last-minute additions or unexpected rejects.

Additional Stationery Needs: Save the Dates, Programs, and More

Emily and Alex needed to think about a lot more stationery in addition to their wedding invites. To let visitors know when their wedding will be and to remind them to mark their calendars, they wanted save-the-date cards. In order to introduce the wedding party and walk visitors through the order of events, they required ceremony programs. Place cards and table numbers were required at the reception to assist visitors in finding their seats. The list appeared to go on forever!

However, Emily and Alex were resolved to approach every task on their stationery checklist with elegance and sophistication. Together with their stationery designer, they produced matching save-the-dates, programs, and other stationery items that matched the style of their invitations and connected the entire wedding theme.

Chapter 5

Ceremony Planning

Emily and Alex were both nervously anticipating their wedding day and simultaneously thrilled with enthusiasm as the sun rose. They had been dreaming of this day since they first met; they would declare their love and devotion to one another in front of their loved ones and closest friends. But there was still a crucial chore to complete before they could say "I do" and walk down the aisle: organizing the ideal wedding.

Creating the Script for Your Ceremony

Writing their ceremony script was the first task on Emily and Alex's checklist for wedding preparation. In addition to wanting their ceremony to be special and unique to them, they also wanted it to be genuine and meaningful, an expression of their love and commitment to one another.

Inspired by weddings they had attended and ceremonies they had seen online, they began by investigating various ceremony styles and customs. They brainstormed ideas on how to include their own personalities and values into the ceremony, taking into consideration components like vows, readings, and customs.

Emily and Alex debated and discussed a lot before deciding on a ceremony script that best reflected their personalities as a pair. They poured their souls out on paper in their vows, committing to one another in an act of love and dedication. They chose readings that really resonated with them; they picked quotes from their favorite novels and poetry that encapsulated their bond. Additionally, they included customs like a handfasting ceremony and the lighting of a unity candle, which served as concrete symbols of their devotion to one another.

Selecting Readings and Music

Choosing readings and music was the next task on Emily and Alex's checklist for ceremony preparation after they finished writing their script. They realized that the appropriate music and words could help establish the mood for the whole day, so they wanted their ceremony to be full of love and emotion.

They began by picking readings that directly spoke to them; they chose verses from books of poetry, novels, and scripture that related to their love journey. They selected readings that matched their ceremony script and gave the proceedings more depth and significance, taking into account elements like tone, duration, and relevancy.

Emily and Alex knew exactly what kind of music they wanted: a selection of modern and classical tunes that complemented each other's styles and established the tone for the day. They picked songs that were special to them and lovely for important events like the unity ceremony, recessional, and professional.

Rehearsal Dinner Details

After deciding on their ceremony's script, readings, and music, Emily and Alex focused on the last task on their checklist: the rehearsal dinner. They wanted their bridal party and family to be able to get together and enjoy before the big day, so they planned a lighthearted and celebratory rehearsal dinner.

For their rehearsal dinner, they decided on a small restaurant with a separate dining area, going for a laid-back atmosphere with great cuisine and plenty of fun. As they were ready to walk down the aisle, they asked their bridal party and close family members to join them for an evening of delicious food and wonderful company. They also exchanged toasts, tales, and encouraging words.

Emily and Alex were excited and looked forward to the next day as the evening was coming to an end and the last of the dessert plates were being taken away. They were aware that their wedding day would be an unforgettable event, marked by a celebration of love and commitment with their closest loved ones.

Chapter 6

Reception Essentials

Emily and Alex found themselves standing hand in hand at the entrance to their reception location, full of excitement and anticipation for the party that lay ahead, as the sun started to drop over the horizon, creating a warm golden glow over the countryside. It was now time to let loose and dance the night away with their closest and dearest. The ceremony had been exquisite and emotional, a genuine representation of their love and dedication to one another. But there were a few crucial reception necessities to attend to before they could begin the celebrations.

Organizing the Layout of the Reception

Organizing the welcome area's layout was the first task on Emily and Alex's checklist. They desired a celebration that was elegant and practical, with lots of space for dining, dancing, and socializing with their guests.

They began by carefully collaborating with their venue planner to ascertain the optimal configuration for their area, considering variables like the number of attendees, the dimensions of the dance floor, and the positioning of essential components like the bar and DJ booth. To guarantee a smooth flow of traffic throughout the evening, they drew out a floor plan, arranging tables, chairs, and other furnishings.

After deciding on a layout, Emily and Alex focused on the interior design. To create a romantic and beautiful environment, they went with a color scheme of soft pastels and gold accents, along with touches of greenery and candles. Together with a group of creative merchants, they brought their idea to reality by renting tables, chairs, linens, and other décor pieces, turning the area into a romantic haven of celebration.

Planning a Menu and Providing Catering Services

Planning the meal and hiring caterers was next on Emily and Alex's agenda for their reception once the setup and décor were finalized. They envisioned their reception as a sensory extravaganza, complete with mouthwatering fare and beverages that would tantalize visitors' palates and leave them feeling full and content.

They began by visiting with several caterers, trying out menus, and going over possibilities for starters, main courses, and desserts. They selected a menu that included a range of selections to satisfy every palate by taking into account variables including dietary restrictions, cultural preferences, and financial limits.

Emily and Alex decided to start with a variety of served hors d'oeuvres and snacking stations that included bite-sized treats like bacon-wrapped dates and gourmet cheeses along with handcrafted charcuterie. They had set meals to choose from for the main course, which included beef tenderloin, vegetarian risotto, and herb-roasted chicken and fish. They then treated their sweet taste to a magnificent dessert buffet, which included enough cakes, pies, and pastries to please even the pickiest eater.

Entertainment: Music, Dancing, and More

After organizing the caterer and creating the meal, Emily and Alex's reception checklist turned to entertainment. With dancing, music, and other activities to keep their guests up late, they envisioned their reception as an endless celebration.

To begin with, they employed a gifted DJ to play music and serve as the event's emcee. After meeting with many DJs to discuss their tastes in music and their ideas for the reception, they finally selected one who could maintain a lively atmosphere on the dance floor and understood their aesthetic.

Emily and Alex wanted to have different kinds of entertainment at their reception in addition to music. They put up a booth where guests could snap goofy photos and make treasured memories by hiring a photo booth provider. To add even more refinement and elegance to the festivities, they also hired a live band to play during dinner.

Speeches and Toasts

With each passing moment, friends and family members showered Emily and Alex with love and joy as the night went on and the music continued to play. They also received poignant speeches and toasts in their honor. They raised their glasses in appreciation of the love and pleasure that permeated the space as they listened to their loved ones share tales, experiences, and wise words.

A highlight of the evening was the speeches and toasts, which gave Emily and Alex the chance to stop and consider the path that had led them to this point in their lives, surrounded by the people they cared about the most. They were thankful for the love and support they had on their wedding day, and they laughed and wept.

And when the last dance was performed and the last toast was given, Emily and Alex experienced happiness and pleasure beyond anything they had ever experienced. They had meticulously prepared the ideal reception—a testament to their love and dedication that would last for years to come.

Thus, my dear readers, Emily and Alex have created the ideal event, complete with a lovely setup, delectable food and beverages, and entertainment that had everyone up dancing all night. But while they continue to celebrate their love and devotion with their closest and dearest, the night is far from done and there are still many memories to be formed and moments to be treasured. Pay attention.

Chapter 7

Decor and Details

Emily and Alex found themselves standing hand in hand in the middle of their reception area as the last rays of daylight faded into twilight and the stars started to twinkle overhead. Vendors were bustling around, putting the final touches on the decor and details that would make their wedding day truly magical. Now that the necessities for the reception were covered, attention could turn to the décor and the elements that would turn their location into a magical haven of celebration and love.

Creating a Cohesive Theme

Developing a unifying theme to unite all elements of Emily and Alex's reception décor was the first task on their checklist for decor and details. Their wedding was to have a unique look and feel, with each component blending together to provide a smooth and beautiful ambiance.

They began by going back over the mood boards and inspiration boards they had made in the early phases of planning their wedding, taking cues from the hues, materials, and themes that really spoke to them. They finally decided on a theme that felt true to who they were as a couple: rustic elegance with a dash of whimsy, taking into account elements like the venue's architecture, the wedding season, and the general feeling they wanted to create.

After deciding on a theme, Emily and Alex started looking for décor pieces that would complete their look. In order to provide warmth and texture, they went with a color scheme of soft neutrals, blush pink, gold accents, and hints of natural wood and flora. They meticulously selected each piece of décor, such as table linens, centerpieces, candles, and signs, to suit their theme and budget, either by renting or buying it.

Tablescapes and Centerpieces

After deciding on a theme, Emily and Alex's checklist for décor and details included creating tablescapes and centerpieces for their reception tables. Their goal was to create tables that were both aesthetically pleasing and useful, with accent pieces that would serve to both help their visitors and improve the overall look.

To add a sense of elegance and romanticism, they began by choosing table linens in gentle tones of blush pink and ivory, along with exquisite lace overlays and gold embellishments. They selected glassware and china in complementary hues and designs, along with elements reminiscent of the past that gave the table settings a sophisticated and charming feel.

Emily and Alex chose to combine candlelight with flower arrangements for their centerpieces. Exquisite bouquets of roses, peonies, and foliage were tucked into gold vases and encircled by votive candles that flickered. They created tablescapes that were both lovely and welcoming by including whimsical elements like old books and little lights.

Personalized Details and DIY Touches

Emily and Alex wanted to include handmade accents and unique embellishments to their reception décor in addition to the primary decor components. They felt that by including these small details, their wedding day would gain even more significance and individuality, becoming genuinely their own.

They began by making personalized place cards and signs that mirrored their theme and style, as well as stationery for their reception. They infused each piece with love and purpose by adding unique elements like monograms and meaningful messages.

Additionally, they asked friends and family for assistance in creating do-it-yourself décor pieces including picture frames, guest book substitutes, and wedding favors. Together, they bonded over glue guns and glitter, spending weekends making and creating as they realized their vision, one handcrafted detail at a time.

Finishing Touches and Day-of Coordination

With the assistance of their day-of coordinator and wedding planner, Emily and Alex found themselves putting the final touches on their decor and decorations as the last days before their wedding day passed by in a blur of excitement and anticipation. They collaborated closely with their group of suppliers to guarantee that every component—including the seating arrangement, table numbers, and welcoming signage—was in place and flawless.

Before anything like this, they had never felt the kind of anxious excitement they had on their wedding morning when Emily put on her bridal gown and Alex adjusted his tie. They were aware that their wedding day would be a celebration of love and commitment spent with the people who had the most meaning in their lives, a day they would never forget.

They realized that their wedding day had exceeded all of their expectations when they entered the reception area and found it transformed into a lovely haven of love and celebration, with every part of the décor lovingly picked and every detail well thought out.

Chapter 8

Legalities and Logistics

On the verge of the most significant day of their lives—their wedding day—Emily and Alex watched as the first rays of dawn peeked over the horizon, casting the world in a gentle golden glow. With hearts full of love and anticipation, they realized that today would be a day full of laughter, joy, and the promise of a lifetime of pleasure spent with each other. It was a day they would never forget. But there were a few crucial legal and logistical matters to attend to before they could exchange vows and walk down the aisle.

Marriage License

Getting a marriage license was the first legal task Emily and Alex had on their list of priorities. They had to get a marriage license from their local government office for their marriage to be recognized by the law. Usually, this process requires completing an application, paying a charge, and presenting identification and age documentation.

Having done their homework beforehand, Emily and Alex were well aware of the steps required to get their marriage license. They scheduled a time to drop in their application in person at the county clerk's office, filled it out in advance, and gathered all the required paperwork.

Excitement and expectation were rising in them as they stood in line, hand in hand, at the county clerk's office. They were eager to begin their new life together as husband and wife and understood that getting their marriage certificate was the last step towards formalizing their relationship.

It was eventually their time at the counter after a short wait. They gave the clerk their application and supporting documentation with big grins on their faces and loving hearts, and the clerk processed them quickly and expertly. And just like that, in a matter of minutes, they had their formal marriage license—a legal document that marked the beginning of their married life and their commitment to one another.

Name Change

Emily's name change was a crucial legal matter that needed to be taken care of. After they were married, she had made the very symbolic choice to adopt Alex's last name as a representation of their unity and dedication to one another.

Emily had to alter her name officially, which meant updating her passport, driver's license, and social security card to reflect her new marital name. Usually, this procedure requires completing an application for a name change, supplying evidence of marriage, and sending the required documentation to the relevant government offices.

Before the wedding, Emily had already begun the process of changing her name by compiling all the relevant papers and completing the forms. While she was aware that it would take some time for her new name to be finalized and appear on all of her documentation, she was prepared to wait in order to become Mrs. Emily Smith in an official capacity.

Timeliness and Logistics

Emily and Alex had to think about the practical aspects of their wedding day as well as the legal aspects of getting married. It was time to make sure that everything went off without a hitch because they had spent months organizing every detail of the day, from the ceremony to the reception.

They drew out a comprehensive timetable for the day that included the whole schedule of activities. To make sure that everyone involved understood where they needed to be and when, they included crucial details like the start time of the ceremony, the arrival of the bridal party, and the beginning of cocktail hour.

Additionally, they worked with their vendors to finalize the setup and arrival timings. To make sure that everyone was in agreement and that everything was ready for the big day, they kept in touch with their videographer, photographer, florist, caterer, and other suppliers.

Emily and Alex were in the midst of a frenzy of activity as they were putting the final touches on their preparations in the last hours before the wedding. Trying to remain composed and in the moment, they double-checked their checklist, verified their reservations, and made any necessary last-minute alterations.

Emergency Kit and Contingency Plans

Emily and Alex assembled an emergency kit and created backup plans to handle any unanticipated situations that could occur on the wedding day.

Essentials including a sewing kit, safety pins, tissues, band-aids, stain remover, pain medicines, and other goods that could come in handy during the day were included in their emergency pack. To ensure that they and the rest of their wedding party were hydrated and fed, they also brought snacks and water bottles.

Emily and Alex had considered a variety of contingency possibilities and created preparations to deal with them. They have three backup plans: one for transportation in the event of a car breakdown, one for adverse weather, and one for any other unforeseen circumstances.

Final Rehearsal and Relaxation

On the eve of their wedding, Emily and Alex met with their bridal party for a last rehearsal to go over the schedule for the ceremony and reception as the sun was setting. They went over every phase of the day, rehearsing their vows, planning entrances and exits, and settling any last-minute issues.

Emily and Alex took some time to decompress and chill down before the big day following the rehearsal. As they ate a nice supper together, they thought back on their journey together and the love and happiness that had carried them this far.

They knew that tomorrow would mark the beginning of a new chapter in their lives—one that would be full of love, laughter, and limitless possibilities—as they fell asleep that night, holding hands. And as they went to sleep, closing their eyes, they couldn't help but be thankful for all of the love and support they had as they started this amazing adventure together.

Chapter 9

The Final Countdown

Emily and Alex were on the verge of the most significant day of their lives—their wedding day—as the first light of dawn bathed the sky in shades of pink and gold. It had been months of preparation, excitement, and expectation, but now the day they had been waiting for had finally arrived. But there were still a few things to do, a few last-minute details to take care of, and a lot of excitement to bask in during the last countdown to their wedding before they could walk down the aisle and exchange vows in front of their loved ones.

Morning Preparations

For Emily and Alex, the day started early; they awoke to soft sunlight coming in through their bridal suite window. They spent some peaceful time together, enjoying the thrill that pervaded the air and the morning's quietness.

Their closest friends and family members were there to support them and provide words of love and encouragement as they prepared for the day. As Alex got ready in his best clothes and smiled eagerly but nervously, Emily was transformed into a picture of bridal beauty by the skillful work of hair and cosmetic specialists.

The Bridal Party

Emily and her bridesmaids got together for the bridal party picture session, the last pre-wedding event, as the morning grew into the midday. As they stood for pictures to immortalize the enchantment and friendship of this unique day, they joked and laughed together, drank champagne, and exchanged tales.

As they got ready for the big day, Alex and his groomsmen had a private time of companionship of their own, cracking jokes and exchanging stories. As they prepared to support and encourage one another as they assisted with their boutonnieres and ties, they stood by Alex's side as he said, "I do."

Final Touches

Emily and Alex were putting the last touches on their wedding day preparations as the hours passed and the ceremony's time approached. They verified that everything was in order and prepared for action by going over their checklist one more time. They made certain that their rings were securely stored in their own ring boxes, prepared for future exchange as a token of their devotion and love.

They stopped for a minute to think back on the path that had led them here, the joy and love, the setbacks and victories, and the many memories they had made together along the way. They were in awe at how much they had changed and matured as a couple and as individuals, and they were incredibly appreciative of the love and support that had seen them through everything.

The Ceremony

Emily and Alex found themselves standing hand in hand at the entrance of their ceremony location, surrounded by the people who meant the world to them, as the day faded into dusk and the sun started to fall below the horizon. It was finally here—the moment they had been waiting for to say "I do."

Their faces were beaming as they walked down the aisle, their eyes fixed on each other and their hearts full of love and anticipation. Following their vows and ring exchange, they sealed their love and devotion with a kiss that warmed everyone's hearts.

A wave of love and thankfulness washed over them as they went back up the aisle as husband and wife, hand in hand and hearts full of happiness. With their "I do" and the start of their new chapter as husband and wife, they had accomplished their goal.

The Reception

Emily and Alex found themselves surrounded by their loved ones once more as the sun sank and the stars started to glitter overhead, this time in celebration of becoming husband and wife. The celebration was a frenzy of love and fun, complete with speeches, dancing, and general mirth that lifted everyone's spirits.

Swaying together in one other's arms as the music played and the outside world faded away, they danced their first dance together as husband and wife. They raised their glasses in celebration of the love that had brought them all together on this special night, sharing smiles and tears as their loved ones took the mike to offer words of love and support.

Emily and Alex found themselves surrounded by a sea of open hearts and happy faces as the night went on and the festivities carried on, each of them a witness to the love and joy that permeated the space. They toasted, laughed, danced, and celebrated, savoring each and every second of this amazing day that they would never forget.

The Afterglow

Finally, alone, Emily and Alex threw themselves in each other's arms and reveled in the aftermath of their wedding day as the last dance sounds died away and the last guests headed home. They thought back on their shared experiences, the love that had encircled them, and the day that had gone by.

They understood that their wedding day was only the start of a journey that would be full of love, joy, and limitless opportunities. With hopes brimming in their hearts, they gazed forward to the future knowing that, as long as they were together, they were prepared to take on any obstacles and experiences that were ahead.

And thus, my dear reader, as husband and wife, Emily and Alex have said "I do" and begun their new chapter in life. But as they go through life together, hand in hand and with hearts full of love, their love story is far from ending. There are still more experiences and memories to be shared.

They know their love is a connection that will never break, a love that will take them through every joy and every difficulty, and a love that will endure a lifetime as they nod off to sleep on their wedding night, surrounded by the warmth and affection of each other's embrace.

Chapter 10

Reflecting on Your Perfect Day

It's normal to experience a range of feelings when the last laughs and sounds of music fade into the night and you find yourselves finally alone, hugged tightly in each other's arms, and enjoying the afterglow of your wedding day. You will always remember your wedding day as a rush of love and happiness, from the thrill of saying "I do" to the delight of celebrating with your loved ones.

The memories that flood your mind as you take a moment to think back on your ideal day may include the way the sunlight danced on the leaves while you exchanged vows, the sound of laughter resounding throughout the dance floor during your first dance, and the overwhelming sense of joy you experienced as you finally realized you were husband and wife.

Give yourself some time to enjoy these recollections, keep them near to your heart, and treasure them for a lifetime. Your wedding day was a celebration of your union, a mark of the relationship you have and the path that took you both to this point. It was a day full of love and happiness, tears and laughter, and moments you will always cherish.

However, while you consider your ideal day, you could also find yourself considering the path ahead of you and the experiences and difficulties you will have as husband and wife. Even if things won't always be simple, you know that you can get through anything as long as you have each other.

Advice for Newlyweds

Here are some tips to help you on your journey as you start this new chapter of your lives together:

1. Have honest and open communication: A happy marriage is built on communication. Spend time talking, sharing ideas

and emotions, and listening to each other with an open mind and heart.

2. Make your relationship a priority. Despite how stressful and demanding life may be, it's crucial to find time for one another. Maintaining the love that brought you together should be your first priority, whether it's a quiet evening at home or a weekly date night.

3. Be patient and understanding: Marriage is a journey, and like any trip, it has its ups and downs. Have patience and understanding. Remember to show each other grace and compassion, especially in trying times, and be patient and understanding with one another.

4. Maintain the romance: Being married does not have to imply that the romance has to end. Maintain the fervor in your partnership by arranging romantic vacations, surprise one another with kind acts, and frequently expressing your love and admiration.

5. Laugh often and don't sweat the small stuff: Life is too short to take things too seriously, therefore laugh a lot and don't

worry about the little things. Be brave enough to enjoy the goofy times, laugh at yourself, and let go of the tiny things that aren't really important in the big picture.

6. Depend on one another and encourage one another's goals: Marriage is a collaboration, thus it's critical to encourage one another's ambitions. Show each other the utmost support and rejoice in each other's accomplishments as though they were your own.

7. Never stop learning and developing as a couple: Marriage is a journey of personal development for each partner as well as for the individual. Never stop learning from one another, from your experiences, and from the outside world. Seize the chance to develop and change as a group.

Your love is the most essential thing of all, so keep it in mind when you think back on your ideal day and look forward to the future. There are no boundaries to what you may do when love is your compass and you have each other by your side. Thus, cling to one another, treasure each instant, and welcome the journey that lies ahead. Congratulations on starting your happily ever after, newlyweds.

May your own love story be filled with as much joy, laughter, and happily ever afters as Emily and Alex's, and may you cherish each moment of your journey together, from the first kiss to the last dance and beyond.

www.ingramcontent.com/pod-product-compliance
Lightning Source LLC
Chambersburg PA
CBHW051659250726
48653CB00007B/2757